SPORTS SUPERSTARS

EILEEN GU

BY INDIA JAMES

TORQUE

TORQUE, AN IMPRINT OF BELLWETHER MEDIA BY FLUTTERBEE

Torque brims with excitement perfect for thrill-seekers of all kinds. Discover daring survival skills, explore uncharted worlds, and marvel at mighty engines and extreme sports. In *Torque* books, anything can happen. Are you ready?

This edition first published in 2026 by Bellwether Media, Inc.

For information regarding permission, write to Bellwether Media, Inc., Attention: Permissions Department, 3500 American Blvd W, Suite 150, Bloomington, MN 55431.

Library of Congress Cataloging-in-Publication Data is available at www.loc.gov or upon request from the publisher.

ISBN: 9798893048377 (hardcover)
ISBN: 9798893049374 (ebook)

Editor: Kieran Downs Designer: Gabriel Hilger

Printed in the United States of America, North Mankato, MN.

TABLE OF CONTENTS

GOLD! 4
WHO IS EILEEN GU? 6
EARLY ON THE SLOPES 8
TROPHIES AND GOLD MEDALS 12
GU'S FUTURE 20
GLOSSARY 22
TO LEARN MORE 23
INDEX 24

GOLD!

It is the women's **halfpipe** final at the 2022 Beijing **Winter Olympics**. Eileen Gu already has two Olympic medals. No one, man or woman, has ever won three in **freestyle** skiing.

Gu races down the halfpipe. She twists and spins in the air. The other scores do not come close. Gu becomes the first person to win three freestyle Olympic medals!

BEIJING 2022
FACTION

WHO IS EILEEN GU?

Eileen Gu is a **professional** freestyle skier. She **competes** for Team China. She skis in many different events.

EILEEN GU

BIRTHDAY	September 3, 2003
HOMETOWN	San Francisco, California
EVENTS	big air, slopestyle, halfpipe
HEIGHT	5 feet 9 inches
JOINED	Team China in 2019

Gu has won competitions all over the world. She is known for launching high off jumps. Gu was the first woman to land a **double cork 1440**.

EARLY ON THE SLOPES

Gu was born to an American father and a Chinese mother. She grew up in the United States. She spent her summers in China.

GU AND HER MOTHER

A Tough Choice

Gu competed in both running and skiing as a kid. She chose to focus on skiing as a teenager.

Gu began skiing when she was only 3 years old. By age 9 she was winning many junior events. She started competing in senior events when she was 13 years old.

Gu started competing in countries outside of the U.S. when she was 14 years old. She won her first **World Cup** event in 2019. She was only 15 years old.

Gu decided to start competing for China in 2019. In 2020, Gu won gold medals at the Winter Youth Olympic Games and at the World Cup.

2019 WORLD CUP

FAVORITES

SPORT OTHER THAN SKIING

running

COLORS

red and black

ACTRESS

Emma Watson

HOBBY

playing piano

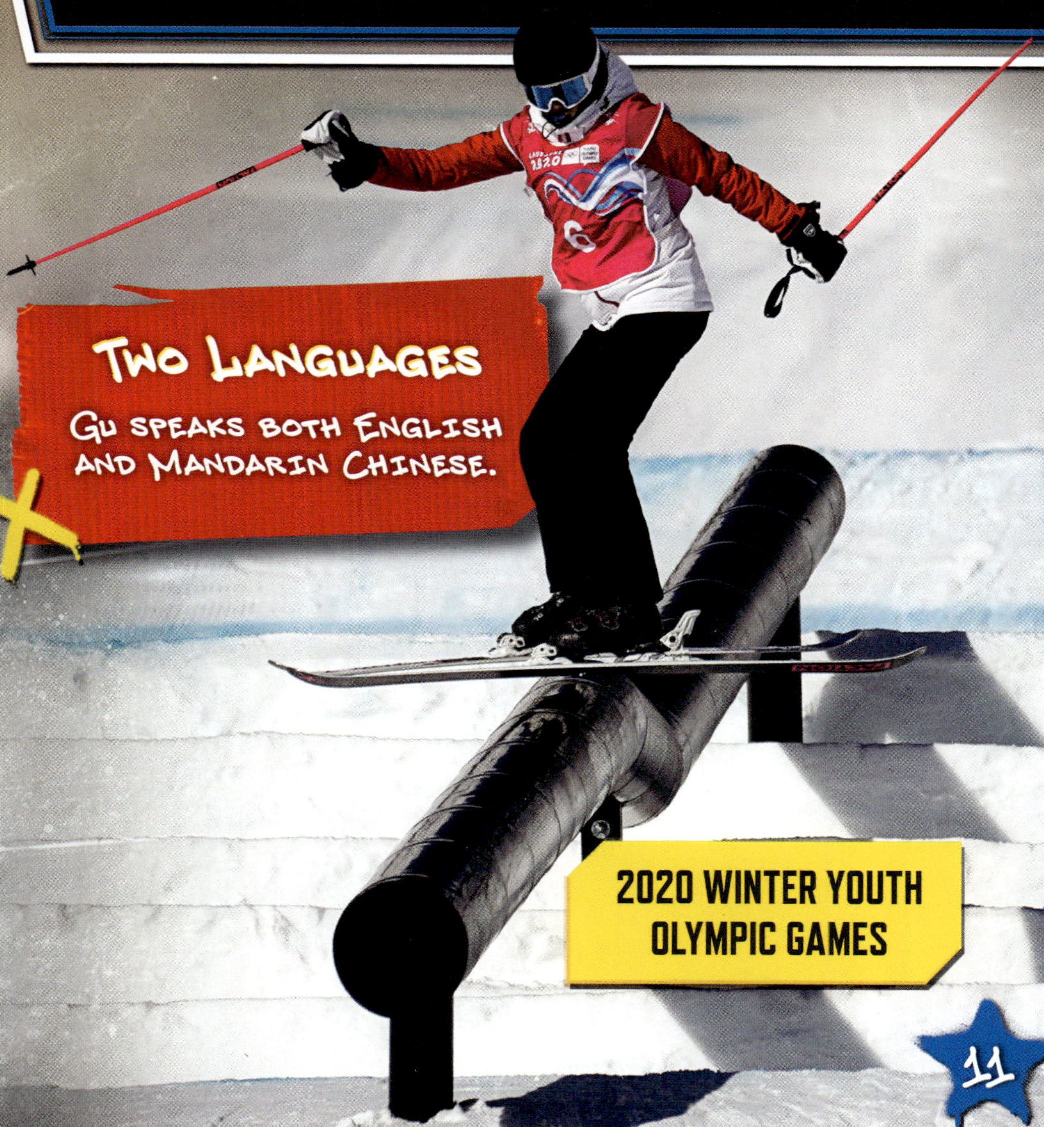

TWO LANGUAGES

GU SPEAKS BOTH ENGLISH AND MANDARIN CHINESE.

2020 WINTER YOUTH OLYMPIC GAMES

TROPHIES AND GOLD MEDALS

2021 WINTER X GAMES

In 2021, Gu competed in her first Winter X Games in Aspen, Colorado. She won gold medals in **slopestyle** and halfpipe. She also won a bronze medal in **big air**. It was the first time that a **rookie** had ever won three medals at the Winter X Games.

She also won medals at five World Cup competitions that season.

Another Name

Gu's name in Chinese is Gu Ailing.

2022 BEIJING WINTER OLYMPICS

The 2022 Winter Olympics in Beijing, China, were Gu's first Olympic games. She won gold medals in big air and halfpipe. She also won silver in slopestyle.

Gu became the youngest person to win an Olympic gold medal in freestyle skiing. She also became the first freestyle skier to win three medals at a single Olympic Games.

EILEEN GU MAP

- 2022 Beijing Winter Olympics, Beijing, China
- Winter X Games, Aspen, Colorado

2022 BEIJING WINTER OLYMPIC MEDALS

Gu started 2023 by winning the World Cup halfpipe event in Calgary, Canada. But she hurt her knee in training. She was not able to compete in the 2023 Winter X Games.

Gu came back to competition later in 2023. She won another World Cup event that December.

2023 WORLD CUP EVENT

2023 WORLD CUP GOLD MEDAL

TROPHY SHELF

2 Olympic gold medals

Olympic silver medal

3 Winter X Games gold medals

Winter X Games bronze medal

Gu won more competitions in 2024. She won her 17th World Cup event at Copper Mountain in Colorado. This gave her more World Cup wins than any other freestyle skier.

Gu was not able to do many events in 2025. She fell during an early event in the Winter X Games. She did not finish her competition.

TIMELINE

2019

Gu wins her first World Cup event

2020

Gu wins two Winter Youth Olympics gold medals

2021

Gu wins three medals at the Winter X Games

2025 WINTER X GAMES

— 2022 —

Gu wins three medals at the Winter Olympics

— 2024 —

Gu wins her 17th World Cup event

GU'S FUTURE

Gu is more than just a skiing champion. She also is a college student, fashion model, and role model. She works to encourage people to live healthy lives by playing sports.

Smart Skier

Gu is a student at Stanford University. She studies physics.

Gu wants to keep skiing in the future. She plans to keep skiing for China, and she wants to ski in the 2026 Milano Cortina Winter Olympics!

GLOSSARY

big air—a competition where the skier performs tricks after launching off a large jump

competes—works for something for which another person is also working

double cork 1440—a trick where the skier turns 4 times in the air

freestyle—related to events based on tricks rather than time

halfpipe—a ski slope that looks like a pipe cut in half

professional—related to a player or team that makes money playing a sport

rookie—a first-year player in a sports league

slopestyle—a competition where the skier performs tricks over various obstacles

Winter Olympics—a worldwide winter sports contest held in a different country every four years

World Cup—an international series of ski races

TO LEARN MORE

AT THE LIBRARY

Abdo, Kenny. *Eileen Gu.* Minneapolis, Minn.: Abdo Zoom, 2023.

Gish, Ashley. *Freestyle Skiing.* Mankato, Minn.: Creative Education, 2026.

Goldstein, Margaret J. *Meet Eileen Gu.* Minneapolis, Minn.: Lerner Publications, 2023.

ON THE WEB

FACTSURFER

Factsurfer.com gives you a safe, fun way to find more information.

1. Go to www.factsurfer.com
2. Enter "Eileen Gu" into the search box and click 🔍.
3. Select your book cover to see a list of related content.

INDEX

big air, 12, 14
favorites, 11
halfpipe, 4, 12, 14, 16
map, 15
profile, 7
slopestyle, 12, 14
Team China, 6, 10, 21
timeline, 18–19
trophy shelf, 17
Winter Olympics, 4, 14, 15, 21
Winter X Games, 12, 16, 18, 19
Winter Youth Olympics, 10, 11
World Cup, 10, 13, 16, 17, 18

The images in this book are reproduced through the courtesy of: Angelika Warmuth/ dpa/ Associated Press, front cover; Aflo Co. Ltd./ Alamy Stock Photo, pp. 3, 14, 15 (2022 Beijing Winter Olympic Medals); Ezra Shaw/ Staff/ Getty Images, pp. 4, 9, 19 (2025 Winter X Games), 21; VCG/ Contributor/ Getty Images, pp. 5, 17, 18; ZUMA Press, Inc./ Alamy Stock Photo, p. 6; Andrew Milligan/ EMPPL PA Wire/ Associated Press, p. 7 (Eileen Gu); somartin, p. 7 (Chinese flag); Xinhua News Agency/ Contributor/ Getty Images, pp. 8, 23; Action Plus Sports Images/ Alamy Stock Photo, p. 10; Xinhua/ Alamy Stock Photo, p. 11 (2020 Winter Youth Olympic Games); lzf, p. 11 (running); BAKOUNINE, p. 11 (Emma Watson); Tiler84, p. 11 (piano); Kelsey Brunner/ The Aspen Times/ Associated Press, p. 12; Sean M. Haffey/ Staff/ Getty Images, p. 13; Andriy Blokhin, p. 15 (Aspen, Colorado); N509FZ/ Wikimedia, p. 15 (Beijing, China); China News Service/ Contributor/ Getty Images, p. 16; Sam Mellish/ Alamy Stock Photo, p. 18 (2020); UPI/ Alamy Stock Photo, p. 19 (2022); Kevin Frayer/ Stringer/ Getty Images, p. 20.